Michel Pleau

Eternity Taking Its Time

Translated by Howard Scott

BookLand
press

Published by BookLand Press
15 Allstate Parkway, Suite 600, Markham, Ontario L3R 5B4
www.booklandpress.com

Printed and bound in Canada.

Front cover photo by Steve Deschênes.

Library and Archives Canada Cataloguing in Publication

Pleau, Michel, 1964-
[Lenteur du monde. English]
  Eternity taking its time / Michel Pleau; translated by Howard Scott.

Poems.
Translation of: La lenteur du monde.
Also issued in electronic format.

ISBN 978-1-926956-31-2
  I. Scott, Howard, 1952- II. Title. III. Title: Lenteur du monde.
English.

PS8581.L42L4613 2012   C841'.54   C2012-904580-2

We acknowledge the financial support of the Government of Canada, through the National Translation Program for Book Publishing for our translation activities. We acknowledge the support of the Canada Council for the Arts, which last year invested $154 million to bring the arts to Canadians throughout the country. We acknowledge the support of the Ontario Arts Council (OAC), an agency of the Government of Ontario, which last year funded 1,681 individual artists and 1,125 organizations in 216 communities across Ontario for a total of $52.8 million. We acknowledge the financial support of the Ontario Media Development Corporation for our publishing activities.

Oh! the clarity of the suns
The embers of childhood

~ Anne Perrier

who knows better than you what you must become
to remain faithful to the being that lives inside you

~ Jean-Noël Pontbriand

TABLE OF CONTENTS

dawn is nothing but childhood
protected by a very old cat
like light under the door

never is the sky slower than
in the water of a fountain
where all the blue in the world is caught

the fire of that time has begun
and memory already
looks like the reflection of a tree
lost in the river

Here

at the hour when memories
raise their lot of ragged voices
I start again to spell the names of flowers
and the visible fire of all things

surprising rust on hands
childhood is that place somewhere
found and habitable
in the miracle of real words

here the silence recalls
a clarity before words

I had no horizon
but in the arms of my mother
even though from her face
fell the first snows of weariness

love was a little fruit
that filled my mouth
and with her eyes
the world found its way again

memory sometimes
alit on my mother's shoulder

then I heard the murmurings
slip from her bird lips
I flew as far as the hollow of her voice
and touched the lightness of time

swaddled in each of her movements
I finally came to rest

A child's drawing

your hands came looking for me
as far as the caverns of the soul

your clouds all bend
to the same side of day
the tulips overflow with their colours
and the sun is like an enigma alone

you have drawn an oak
that stirs in my heart
I hear the rippling
of your footsteps in mine

I listen inside me to your snow birds

your wax night is so light

your spirals bring back in me the gods
from another summer sculpted by fire

you have drawn the wind
that alights among the stones
and takes up all the space

time clings to the branches
and touches me like never

over the mountains the moon
looks like lost children

I would love to live in your houses
where the windows
are lovely nests of light

you have imagined huge seagulls
that the sky is preparing to leave
for the mirror of light embers

fresh clarity of wool and straw
you cross the foliage of a signature
forgotten at the foot of the page

on the other side of your images
the wind is preparing the world
for fires other than boredom

and while a raft of sand
glides slowly on the river
soothing the blue walls of the soul
under the apple tree
the apples go on dreaming
of landscape transparency

you watch eternity
taking its time

the gaze is patient
that untangles stones
deep in sleep

the bird is no higher than memory
and you are there unfinished with waiting

your hands watch over the world

your footsteps are lost
in the chalk of days
you still throw stones
toward the future that flows far away

a strange glow alights
on that other apple tree from another season

a transparent cloth
covers the name of things

it's summer
on the line the sheets grow bored

dawn is a boat
from which rises the wind of the soul

all dreams begin for you
in this square of desires
unknown to ashes

you have the easy laugh of the mountains
and a voice calmer than grass

the hours in your hands
no longer hesitate to dig
the soil of ploys

do you really know the night
adorable sleeper of sand

do you know the wet innocence of flowers
the embers of a field of wheat
when vegetable sun
kneads the bread that feeds the heart

the windows of childhood
prepare the trees to age

a perfect clarity
settles on the words
like a basket of snow

but the heart
is a candle of blood
that can burn out tomorrow

all those branches
that bear the weight of heaven
you first warmed them
in the hollow of your palm
little forest where the lines
of wandering intertwine

what is there behind that domain
what landscape lies there

a slow snow
teaches you the age of the earth

the birds rediscover the wind of winging it
as if they were born
to stitch the sky

in this carbon paper night
the moon is a sack of light
right in the middle of the world

First-love poem

I remember her face
from the first forest
hidden in childhood
and her daisy lips
moving toward the unknown

can you imagine a light lovelier
than the long long time
climbing to the self
and memory
building itself a nest
for the possible next day

because wind blows through memories
a wind of clearing and girl
lost in the woods of origins

The sun of old

the sun of old inhabits memory

under the lament of a world about to be born
are revealed the secrets
of blood and of love

and so birth
ploughs the soul

behind the mountains
dawn resembles only its reflection

the first wind
continues its slow march to me
and slips the name of things
into the hollow of my hands

At the windows

today at the windows
lingers the cold interior of the landscape

why this familiar snow
in the depths of memory
and the full echo
in the footsteps of the dead

I leave a lamp at night
draw fragile frontiers
space is a hand
caressing the world

The mornings of eternity

when I blow on the flames
a trembling flower leaves me
beautiful memory
too slow to stand

but they are sweet the mornings of eternity
when dreams tremble again
in the simplicity of movements
and the fulfilment of fruits

then I go out of myself

outside the light
is an ancient perfume
become desire

it is a time of crazy foliage
bending over the beginning of things

The old photos

in the old photographs
the eyes see nothing
but the other side of the world

and also the earth pierced by roses
when they want to look like the sun
and become the fur of a landscape
slow as a lantern

the light is heavy
when it warms the fruits
and takes the shape of an orange

on the old photographs
the night is never alone

in the ballyhoo of memories
the miracle of a flower
caught in the traps of beauty

The slowness of the world

we have received our soul irrevocably
and the night takes us here and there
to the forests that open our eyes

what we have to learn
to be born from the belly of a tree
and promise childhood to come back

the shadow at the end is clothing
taken off us

but the sun comes out of the earth
and separates us from forgetting
it waits until rise within
the words chained to the shores
of a distant meeting

the silent breath of things
gathers around it
the place and the beginning

and yet I'd like to redo the landscape
with the patience of my hands

time has not yet found its dwelling

my past has forever
been used as a nest of words

but this morning I hear
passers-by and their insect footsteps
life scattered on the shoulders
I know all the transparency
accumulated in things

everything is far from here
when I take refuge in the words
that have not yet dreamed

memory is a broken window
in the house of childhood

it was summer
with its share of scribbling and rain

I was at the age
where you don't yet touch time

I didn't know all the bread I would have to break
to escape the dictates of the gods

faithful in remembering our shadows
they say the sun carries
in itself the breathing of light

for anyone who knows how to close their eyes
they say that the hand touches the soul

they also say that fountains
are the fruits of little girls that are crying
when the lamps are turned off too quickly

the streetlamps know nothing of the stars
and yet continue to give them the sky

what remains of the tree that taught me the wind

the echo of origins
fell asleep somewhere
in the snow of dreams

at night
I throw myself into the warm straw of dreams
like a fruit
overcoming death

that taught me the stained glass of sleep
or else the first landscape
forever deep in my eyes

I walk in me
and look for the simple words
from another time
where boredom was a boat
to cross the night

my mother gathered the wind
and gave it to us to drink

if you've never drunk the wind
you know nothing of childhood

it is the origin that is being written
when we meditate
beside a candle

more than ever
we resemble our shadow
and the words again become visible

the flame is patient
feeds on our body

at night splendour calls us
and we step forward in our hearts
as silence would between stones

repeating branches of the world
I climb into your dreams

I was born of a fatigue
from which you only heal slowly

dark wrenching night
the sun is a stone
that has rejected death

a tree is forever
the reflection of another tree

never have I come as close to myself
as in that instant when my fingers
outlined a new world

in spite of ignorance of words
I had the weight of my presence

I talk too fast sometimes
I speak above things

I hear the world
spread out like old rain

how to be of a single piece
while trees crumble
as they near the heavens

how huge black pudgle
not to take itself for its shadow

pure May morning
you protect the slowness
light is a little lighter on things
you reveal the dazzling blossoming
that hides the old poems

and another clarity
is spreading anew across the earth
unknown to me
the maternal roundness of the word
and the unmentionable milk of embrace

but it is with a fertile voice
that I move quiet to myself

High winds

you never know
what remains of the storm
after it has spilled
its overflow of lies
even into the abodes

nor how the lamps
drink from memory

and then comes the moment
when the night thinks
only of touching the name of things
to become the pond
that claims the abandoned world

Friday

Friday
is a day more ancient than the others
and recalls the perfect luminosity
of the end of classes

in me the words of a little girl
and my heart groggy with so much love

finally came the soothing of the hours
and the crazy harvest of dreams

the sky gave me a glimpse of real birds
I was no longer alone
I touched the space beside me

How do you say it

how do you say it
the uncertain glow rising

it's spring
the eternal lips of lovers
heal time

how to say the seedings of day
and soul from the other shore

before the snow soothed the landscape
and the statues
were little museums of obscurity

but here a sky of chickadees
leans against the blue of the air

fleeting is the shadow
under the words of lovers

now that the rain
is more naked than summer
and the river is long with its memory
I would like to come back
to the first gaze that saved me

how do you speak
despite the silence that covers the earth

from afar I saw that landscape
whose echo brings back the light

how do you say that spring

in all places I ask my way
among the bushes where dawn lingers

we are all born in the month of May
but how do you say
just when the sky
unfolds above the trees

Six o'clock in the morning

is it the same light as yesterday
that settles on things
or rises in itself

for a moment the sun hopes
speaking in us
leaving the sky for the arms of a woman
again becoming the dream stone
in the pockets of a child

when then the sun all to yourself

Becoming

when we push the door open
finally come out of the shadow
stuck to our skin

we find under our feet
the clarity needed to move forward

the space is huge
when the house is burning behind us
when we've stopped gathering the ashes

it's then that the wind
gives sky to the trees
and we want to become ourselves
wind sky and trees

it's then that we want to become
really become our actions
become becoming
visible at the end of our hands
at the end of day
at the end of the elsewhere
where life has already begun

ABOUT THE AUTHOR

Michel Pleau has devoted his life to literature. The recipient of many awards, this poet gives lectures, takes part in public readings, leads creative writing workshops, mentors young poets in their writing process and contributes to several reviews, in-  cluding *Possibles* and *Art LeSabord*. Michel Pleau is literally present in the Quebec landscape as well: an island in the Caniapiscau reservoir in the north of Quebec bears the name of his collection *La traversée de la nuit*. Winner of the 2007 Résidence d'écriture Québec-Paris, he won his first Governor General's Award in 2008 for *La lenteur du monde* published by Les Éditions David.

ABOUT THE TRANSLATOR

Howard Scott is a Montreal literary translator originally from Ontario. In 1997, he received the Governor General's Translation Award for his translation of Louky Bersianik's *The Euguelion*. He has translated many books of poetry, fiction and non-fiction, often in collaboration with Phyllis Aronoff. In 2001, they won the Quebec Writers' Federation Translation Award for *The Great Peace of Montreal of 1701* by Gilles Havard and in 2009 they were shortlisted for the Governor General's Literary Award. He is a past president of the Literary Translators' Association of Canada.